XXIInd Dr. M.A. Ansari Memorial Lecture

THE BRITISH HISTORICAL CONTEXT AND PETITIONING IN COLONIAL INDIA

XXIInd Dr. M.A. Ansari Memorial Lecture

THE BRITISH HISTORICAL CONTEXT AND PETITIONING IN COLONIAL INDIA

Majid Siddiqi

Introduction by
S. Inayat A. Zaidi

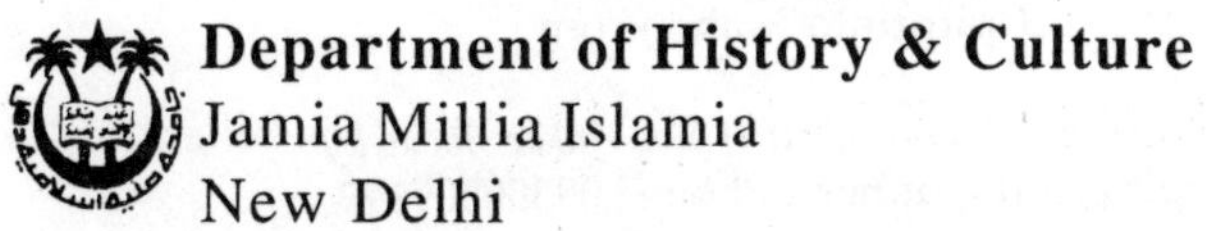

THE BRITISH HISTORIAL CONTEXT AND PETITIONING IN COLONIAL INDIA

First Published, 2005

ISBN 81-87879-50-5

Published by
AAKAR BOOKS
28-E, Pocket-IV, Mayur Vihar Phase-I, Delhi-110 091
Phone : 011-2279 5505 Telefax : 011-2279 5641
E-mail : aakarb@del2.vsnl.net.in

Typeset at
Arpit Printographers
arpitprinto@yahoo.com

Printed in India on behalf of M/s Aakar Books by
Arpit Printographers, Phone : 09350809192

Dedicated to

the memory of Shaheed Bhagat Singh

who sacrificed his life for the

freedom of the Nation

Dr. Mukhtar Ahmad Ansari (1880-1936)

ACKNOWLEDGEMENT

In the series of publication, the Dr. M.A. Ansari memorial lecture on Petitioning in British India is the third. For publication grant, I am thankful to the former Vice Chanceller Syed Shahid Mahdi. I am also thankful to my colleagues for their keen interest in getting this lecture published.

Sunita Zaidi
Head
Dept. of History & Culture

Introduction

*S. Inayat A. Zaidi**

With progress in the civilization of a society, certain norms and etiquettes became an important part of the social, cultural and political life. The word *arzdasht* or petition is indicative of the progress that began to mark the difference between inferior and superior; junior and senior; and subordinate and master.

To know the origin and etymology of the word *arzdasht*, one has to peep into the past. *Arzdasht* is a combination of two words, *i.e., arz* and *dasht, Arz* is an Arabic word, while *dasht* has its roots in the Persian language. *Arz* means submission or filing of an application,[1] while *dasht* means "to have" or "to possess."[2] Thus the synthesis of these words, *i.e., arz* and *dasht* means "to possess a request". This is simply the dictionary meaning and literary rendering of two words which became one *i.e., arz dasht*. Thus, the word *"arz"* reached Persia, where, joining with the Persian word *"dasht"*, it headed towards India in one form, *i.e., "arz dasht"*.

Arzdasht acquired a distinctive nature in Indian society. Ali Akbar Dehkhuda points out that in India, *arzdasht* was an expression used by Princes and nobles in place of 'His Excellency' and by youngsters to their elders.[3]

---

* Professor in the Department of History and Culture, Jamia Millia Islamia.

Two forms of its usages have been deciphered in India. In one sense, whenever a junior, inferior or subordinate person addresses his senior, superior or master respectively, the words *arz* or *arzdasht* are used in an ordinary manner while in the other sense, it is used in the sense of petition. Technically, a person representing redressal of his grievance or seeking a favour would use this word, and the document in which he expresses his desire for the same, is known as *arzdasht* or *petition*.

Other synonyms for *arzdasht* are *arznamcha, iltimas* and *wajib ul arz*. Abul Fazl used the word *arznamcha*[4]. Iltimas and *Wajib ul arz* also appear to denote 'petition' in documents of the seventeenth century.[5] However, in the vernacular languages, the corrupt forms of *arz dasht* or *arz's* are *ardas, arj* or *arjee.*[6] *Ardas* is used for prayer; it is also used to denote prayer to the Guru by the sikh devotees; similarly, *arj or arjee* implies a request by an inferior to a superior. If the position of the inferior is not accepted, then the petition or *arzdasht* is not entertained. An interesting evidence of this nature is worth citing here. In 1782, when Monsr. de Chemont refused to write to Hyder Ali in the form of an *arzdasht*, preferring to correspond with him in the same manner as Mons. Duplex had with Chanda Saheb, the Nawab refused to receive any letter other than that written in the style of *arzee* or petition.[7]

The references of *arzdasht* are found with the foundation of the Delhi Sultanate. The important texts containing *arzdashts* are Amir Khusrau's *Ijaz-i Khusravi* (1292 A.D.); Ain ud Din Abdullah Mahru Multani's *Tarassul Ain ul Mulki Insha-i Mahru* (1362 A. D.); Khwaja Imamuddin, popularly known as Mahmud Gawan's *Manazir ul Insha* (1481 A.D.); Mir Abul Qasim Khan Namakin's *Munshat-i Namakin* (1598 A.D.); Harkaran's *Insha-i Harkaran* and *Zubdat Insha* (1617 A.D)[8]

We also come across references to the *arzdasht* in the chronicles. Moreover, the original copies of the *arzdashts* can be found in the Andhra Pradesh State Archives, Hyderabad, Rajasthan State Archives, Bikaner. In Bikaner, besides Persian *arzdashts*, Rajasthani *arzdashts* are also in abundance.

The *arzdashts* were classified according to the nature of

their contents. There was a separate office, and the officer dealing with these petitions was known as *arz-begi*[9] who used to receive, and present these to the concerned authorities and then note the decision. The summary of the petition was known as *Yad dashti* (memorandum).[10]

The petitions were placed before the emperors. *Tuzuk-i Jahangiri*, an autobiograpy of Emperor Jahangir contains many petitions. A few are cited here to illustrate the nature and contents of the petitions submitted to Jahangir. When Inayat Khan, *bakhshi* of the *ahadis* fell critically ill, he sent a petition to the Emperor desiring to return to Agra from Gujarat.[11] His petition was accepted.

The Princes were also subject to the permission of the Emperor for celebrating functions. Prince Shahjahan petitioned the Emperor from Ujjain to permit him to celebrate the birthday of Aurangzeb. Permission was granted to him.[12] A senior noble, Khan-i Dauran's petition to seek retirement from the military service is reproduced here for the interest of the readers. Jahangir writes, 'At this time a petition came from Khan-i Dauran, stating that: "Your Majesty, from the perfection of kindness and knowledge of his worth, had appointed to the government of Thatta (Sind) an old slave, notwithstanding his great age and weak sight. As this weak old man was exceedingly bent and decrepit, and had not in him the ability to exert himself or to ride, he prays that he may be excused military service, and that he may be enrolled in the army of prayer." At his request, I ordered the chief Diwans to confirm him in the *pargana* of Khushab, with a revenue of 3,000,000 of dams, and which he for a long time had held as *Tankhwah jagir*, and which had become peopled and cultivated, by way of providing for his expenses, so that he might pass his time in easy circumstances.'[13]

Arzdasht or petitions of the officials which simply communicate or report the matter to the emperor or other higher authorities are numerous. A petitioner reports on 13th November, 1637 to Emperor Shah Jahan the activities of Nawab Shaista Khan and Prince Aurangzeb who were posted in the Deccan.

The Nawab met the Prince in the Ghusl Khana (private tent) and the Prince permitted the Khan to sit in his presence. Shaista Khan presented *Nazr* (gifts); he was followed by Bihar Singh and Jag Deo. After about two hours, the Prince retired and Nawab Shaista Khan and the others returned to their respective tents. The Prince honoured the Nawab with a few dishes of his table, through his serving eunuch, upon which the Nawab gave rupees two hundred and a shawl to the bearer.[14]

From one memorandum, it is evident that matchlockmen in the service of Mir Momin represented to the Pay-Master-General for not receiving their pay for a period of six months. They stated the reason for not getting salary as their descriptive rolls and statement of accounts not having been received from the Imperial court. The Pay-Master-General gave orders for part payment of two months' salary.[15] Similarly, a joint petition, dated 21 December, 1661, submitted by Mani Ram Hazari, Guru Das and Man Singh, the *Sadiwals* stationed at the fort of Aurangabad against *Qiladar* Sultan Quli Beg, was filed for appropriation of the salaries of the garrison, causing the soldiers great hardship and distress.[16]

We also come across some petty servants who petitioned against the harassment caused by their superior officials. In July 1659, Chhajju Beg, an *ahdi* attached to the supply Department in Deccan, petitioned Murshid Quli Khan, *Mir Bakhshi*, to direct the Deputy *Bakhshi* to sign his muster-roll (salary voucher). He, on account of complying with the order to perform special duty for collecting *peshkash* (tribute) from the *zamindar* of Ambar *pargana,* could not reach in time for personal verification. Action was taken and an order was issued to the deputy *Bakhshi* of the *ahdis* to comply with the petitioner's request.[17]

In 1661, an ordinary employee like Fathullah, a mason posted at the mausoleum of Rabia Daurani, petitioned for the monthly payment of salary which he did not receive.[18]

We also come across petitions which were rejected by the authorities. When a petition dated 16 January, 1671, filed by Bhopal Jadun, father-in-law of Jaswant Singh, praying that as the scale of the salary granted to him was not in consonance with the scale of other Rajput *Mansabdars* residing in Hindustan, most of whom were favoured with six-monthly, seven-monthly and eight-monthly scale of salary, he might also be granted the six-monthly scale enabling him to live without anxiety, was put up, it was rejected.[19]

It is significant to note that some petitions submitted to the persons of royal family members or people of high status, were gold-flecked or gold sprinkled. It is also pointed out how a petitioner, whose petition was once rejected, tried to prevail upon the Emperor through some influential lady to get favours. This kind of petition was submitted by Abdulla to Nawab Bai (consort of Aurangzeb) on 30th January, 1669. He prayed that after the demise of his son, the post of *faujdar* of *pargana* Arandole be granted to him, but when the matter was sumbitted to the Emperor, it was rejected. The petitioner, owing to the indigent condition of his family, requested the Emperor that he might be appointed at Burhanpur. The Emperor ordered Sazawar Khan, an official, to submit a report in this connection.[20]

Some petitions filed or presented personally by the ordinary people are referred to in the sources. Italian traveller Manucci took out stock of human fat from a corpse of a muslim for medicinal purpose at Lahore. This act of Manucci was considered sacrilege of the dead and also against Islam. The relatives of the dead represented to Mughal officer Fidae Khan against Manucci and demanded punishment for him, but the official did not entertain their petition. Thereafter, they decided to present their petition to the Emperor. Clad in mourning, they went to the Imperial court. But the Emperor without paying heed, dismissed their petition with a brief remark '*Quziya-i-zamin, be sar-e-zamin* (cases about land are settled on the land it self)[21].

Similarly in 1586, when Raja Udai Singh of Jodhpur escheated the villages of the charans, two thousand charans committed suicide. One of the well-known charans, Dursa Ara stabbed himself in his own neck and petitioned Emperor Akbar. All the Rajputs present in the court criticised the act of Udai Singh, but the Emperor seems to have avoided taking any action against the Raja. He said that the name of such a person should not be cited and made a sarcastic remark calling him Mota Raja.[22]

The petitions of redressing their grievances are also in extant from the successor states of the Mughal empire. We come across a petition of a woman who presented her case to the Raja of Bikaner in 1797 A. D. She submitted that she had agricultural land (Khet) shared by her relations. The land was mortgaged to a carpenter. Even after paying back the debt by the woman, she was not allowed to plough her land. Against of it, she presented her case to the Raja who ordered that no body will hinder in the work of the lady and a weak should not be harassed by a powerful.[23]

The filing of petitions had become so common in the public that even in the folk tales, we come across the filing of petitions to the higher authorities to redress their grievances. In western Rajasthan, a tale of a ghost Badshah is popular. When the wife of a certain baniya, Thobhan Baniya, was abducted and could not be traced, the Bania petitioned the night court of ghost *Badshah*. In the night, the Bania appeared in the court of the *Bhut Badshah* himself. The *Badshah* immediately enquired of the matter from his courtier, and learned that the wife of the Baniya had been abducted by Abdul *bhut* of village Bisalnagar. Immediately Abdul *bhut* was summoned to the court, but he refused to acknowledge his crime. After a thrashing, he admitted his wrongdoing, the abducted lady was procured and was restored to the *Bania*.[24]

Thus, it is obvious that in the pre-colonial period, there was a well established and sophisticated mechanism to file petitions to the superior authorities. These petitions were classified as per their subjects and to deal with them, there was a separate office and officer.

This window was open to the people to ventilate their grievances and also to express their feelings. It was a way to have direct communication and to remain in touch with the people, and the state considered its duty to meet the expectations of the people.

The petitions have philological significance. The vocabulary, verbose style of writing and expression show the inferior and the superior positions between the petitioners and the authorities. From the language of the petition one can see how much a petitioner can compromise with his personal dignity?

The feelings of the petitioners varied in context, time and space. Basic difference in the feelings of the petitioners was that the pre-colonial rulers treated petitioners as their own people, and the latter too had the same feeling of considering the rulers their own, but during the colonial period this kind of feeling was missing among both. The petitioners were conscious about the feeling of otherness for the colonial power and the latter too had the same feeling of 'otherness' for their colonial subjects.

REFERENCE

1. J.M. Cowan, (ed.), *Arabic-English Dictionary*. 3rd edition, (Printed India), 1976, p-608.
2. F. Steingass, *A comprehensive Persian English Dictionary,* Delhi, 1973, p-498.
3. Ali Akbar Dehkhuda, *Lughatnama* ed.33, 1341, Tehran, p-170.
4. Abul Fazl, *Ain-i-Akbari,* ed. Sir Syed Ahmad Khan, Delhi, 1855, p-193. Tr. H. Blochmann, Vol. I, p-273. Statements of sums forwarded to court by the collectors of the Imperial domain.
5. Yusuf Husain Khan, ed., *'Selected Documents of Aurangzeb's Reign* (1659-1706 A.D.), Hyderabad, 1958, pp. 3, 67-68, 80-81, 82-83, 84-85.
6. H.H.Wilson's *A Glossary of Judicial and Revenue Terms and Useful Words Occurring in Official Documents Relating to the Administration of the Government of British India From the Arabic, Persian, Hindustani, Sanskrit, Hindi, Bengali, Uriya, Marathi, Guzarathi, Telugu, Karnataka, Tamil, Malyalam and other languages,* Delhi, second ed. 1968, p. 33.
7. Hobson-Jobson-*A Glossary of Colloquial Anglo-Indian Words and Phrases, and of kindered Terms, Etymological, Historical, Geographical and Discursive* by Col. Henry Yule and A.C. Burnell Delhi, ed. 1968, p. 960.
8. See, S.I.A. Tirmizi, 'Medieval Indian Diplomatics', Presidential Address, Medieval India Section, *Indian History Congress,* 43rd session.
9. Mohd. Ziauddin Ahmed Shakeb, ed., *Mughal Archives,* vol. I, Hyderabad, 1977, p. 93; Wilson's *Glossary,* p. 33.

10. Some detailed information undergoes a process, and extract of that detailed information is designated as *Yaddasht*. For details of the process, see, Yusuf Husain Khan, ed., *Documents of Shah Jahan's Reign*, Hyderabad, 1950, pp. X-XI.
11. *Tuzuk-i Jahangiri*, Ed. Syed Ahmad Khan, Ghazipur, 1863, p. 248.
12. Ibid, p. 251.
13. Ibid, p. 275.
14. Yusuf Husain Khan, *Selected Documents of Shah Jahan's Reign*, pp.28-29. Prince Aurangzeb bestowed on the Nawab a *Saropa* (robe of honour) and *Char qab* (robe of Turkish regal design), two horses of Iraqi breed and a bejewelled *Jambwah* (dagger).
15. Ibid, pp. 117-18.
16. Yusuf Husain Khan, *Documents of Aurangzeb's Reign*, pp. 39-40.
17. Ibid, p. 3
18. Ibid, pp. 20-21
19. Ibid, p. 84. On 1 June, 1671, Siddi Jauhar who was in distress because of his transfer, petitioned to be posted at Burhanpur so that he might be able to settle the affairs of his *jagir* properly. But his request was rejected by the the Emperor. Ibid, pp. 97-8.
20. For gold flecked petition, see, Yusuf Husain Khan, *selected documents of Aurangzeb's Reign*, pp. 68-9, 85.
21. Niccolao Manucci, *Storia-do-Mogor*, Tr. by William Irvine, Calcutta, reprint 1967, Vol. II, part II, p.p 197-98.
22. Raja Udai Singh was physically very fat, thus Akbar's remark carries dual meaning. In the literal sense 'mota' means 'fat' and in the sarcastic sense 'powerful'. However, after this, the Raja was known by the name of Mota Raja. See Shyamal Das, *Vir-Vinod*, Delhi 1986, Bhag II, p. 816.
23. *Kaghdo-re Bahi*, N. 10, Samvat 1854, Rajasthan State Archives, Bikaner. There is huge collection of *arzdasht* and *yad dashtis* in Persian and Rajasthani. Descriptive lists of some have been printed and published by the Archives.
24. *Vishambhara*, Sampadak: Vidhya Dhar Shastri, 1965, vol. 1-4, p. 58.

The British Historical Context and Petitioning in Colonial India

Majid Siddiqi

Mr. Vice-Chancellor, colleagues, and friends,

I am delighted to have been invited to deliver the XXII Dr. M.A. Ansari memorial lecture. I consider it a unique privilege that Jamia has accorded to me and I hope that what I have to say will be of some interest to the academic community.

The audience may have noticed that in the title of this lecture the conjunction 'and' has been used (rather than a possible 'of' or 'a') towards the British historical context and petitioning in colonial India. This is deliberate and is intended to demarcate the British historical context from petitioning in colonial India. It is hoped that by doing this we will arrive at some tentative conclusions about the contemporaneous phenomenon of early nationalism in India, conclusions that might enable us to review the latter not merely as derivative from the impact of European ideologies and within the boundaries of empire, or, again, merely as responsive to the challenge of colonial subjection. Rather, it will be our endeavour to describe how petitioning in colonial India was a process integral to the emergence of both early nationalism and the nascent nation-state. We believe that this may be done best by describing and reflecting upon petitioning in India and comparing its many similarities with petitioning in Britain, to highlight the significantly divergent implications for characterizing the historical body-politic in each of the two interrelated but vastly different historical contexts of India and Britain.

PETITIONING IN COLONIAL INDIA

It is established historiographic wisdom that when the power and responsibility of the colonial state was transferred from the East India Company to the Crown, British policy in India was marked by a gradualism conditioned in the main by the reaction of the rulers to the traumatic turbulence of the Great Rebellion of 1857. Consequently, when dissension from power and political opposition is studied or researched, it is always against such a backdrop. In the historical period associated with the second half of the nineteenth century, even revolts are assigned their duly fixed place, episodic as these indeed were, centred upon "local" causes. Between 1860 and 1885, the indigo rebellion, the Mappila uprisings, the Padna riots, and the Deccan agrarian resistance are thus riveted to their specific provenance. The "alternative" history to this has traced the growth of political associations among the Indian intelligentsia from the early 1850s. In their respective ways, the British India Association, the Madras Mahajan Sabha, the Poona Sarvjanik Sabha, and numerous other organizations of the period led to (or seem to lead to) the founding of the Indian National Congress in 1885.[1] Whenever the question of the study of Indian mentalities under colonial rule has been broached, invariably the answer seems to have lain in peasant attitudes or in the class-based responses of the nascent nationalist intelligentsia to colonial rule.[2] Lately, in view of the Orientalist determination of the initial decades of British rule in India in the eighteenth century, and probably even as a response to the two main types of the straight-jacketing of political Indian history just referred to, the question "who represents the Indian past?" has been raised.[3] The question has been answered but only parochially, on the basis of sectional assertions of social entities such as caste groups or individual biographies or recapitulations of nativistic histories. Such accounts, obviously, can only be regional or particularistic, therefore the histories that these seek to "represent" or explicate are also partial and can in no sense be described as "Indian".[4]

In whatever manner it might be argued that "total history" is in any case not (and never was) possible, and that the history of society in the period of emergent nationalism in India must, after all, be a "constructed" history, the question would still remain that if the history of Indian society under British rule is to be written, it must be done with archives or categories of narration and analysis that are apposite to the task. Otherwise we would be left with the grotesque paradox that is characterized by the insistent use of the adjective "colonial" as in colonial Malabar, Bengal, "North India" etc., but less and less as in colonial India. Thus, while colonial regions have in the recent past proliferated in Indian history, yielding a variety of "colonial" social structures, colonial India seems to have disappeared behind this multitude of competing "colonial" (sub-) societies.[5] Without attempting to set the balance right and restore "British rule" and/or "colonialism" to its rightful place in the historical writings on India's recent past, this lecture, more modestly, and among other things, seeks to reflect upon attitudes, mentalities and political dispositions India-wide as these may be found in the petitioning process.

Petitions to the colonial government of British India were addressed by people from all walks of life and on a vast variety of issues. The very heterogeneity of the issues, the spatial distribution of their provenance, and the fact of their always being concerned, directly or tangentially, with the question of British rule and the manner of its functioning, allows us to comprehend the workings of Indian society at both levels, of mentality and of ideology. In their interaction with colonial rule, the petitioners revealed, directly, or subtly, their deepest fears, hates, loyalties and anxieties, their emotions in the widest possible range of inflexion and nuance, even entire cultural systems, of concord and discord, unities and fissures, legitimation and dissent. The colonial bureaucracy, for its part; recorded these and reacted in every single moment of its own contemporaneity to the exigencies of every fresh instance of a representation made, setting up and continually calibrating the terms of significance and according a routine pace to the many issues of everyday life that characterized the flow of events in colonial India.

Let it be said at the very outset that the early history of British rule in India had involved the use of unfettered force and guile and the rejection and suppression of many a petition. As the regime acquired a steadiness of character, it was then, and mainly for reasons of administrative convenience, that the routinized form of petition-making was instituted. Its origin lay in a military despatch of the East India Company's Court of Directors in 1787 that advised its civil and military servants to address the issues of concern or complaint through the government in India.[6] A half-century later, in 1814, the Court directed the government of the Company to retain a "Memorial" or an "Address" for 20 days for perusal and preliminary scrutiny before forwarding it on.[7] By 1848 the practice of addressing government in a printed form (as had been adopted by the Madras government) was discontinued.[8] By that date not only the servants of the Company, but large numbers of the subject Indian population had begun addressing the government on a series of diverse subjects. Usually these petitions were dealt with at the regional level of their orientation, by the local government. But by the middle of the nineteenth century, as colonial rule entered the period of laissez faire, the compelling necessities of better political management, amidst the suppression of revolts, and the carrying out of predatory wars of annexation, determined

> Our anxious desire to avoid all interference with the privilege of addressing memorials to us, but we must at the same time, intimate our expectation that Memorials will be addressed to us only on matters which immediately affect the interests of the (individual) Memorialist.

Memorials and petitions, however, were expected to be polite.

> We need scarcely repeat on this occasion (1848) the injunctions heretofore given that memorials shall be received and forwarded to us only when couched in temperate and respectful language.[9]

This was repeated in 1867 in the rule governing the discretionary power of Indian administration to withhold the transmission of any petition to Britain. The language deployed was not to be "disrespectful" and "improper". At the same time, the broadening of the terms of the acceptance of petitions led by 1850 to including petitions in the vernacular language and accompanying translations were first encouraged and then, by 1867, made mandatory upon the Government of India.[10]

We have mentioned the colonial state's explicitly repeated assertions requiring a polite mode of address in the petitions to draw attention to the legitimate inference that we may make that at least the implied questioning of British rule had already by the middle of the nineteenth century, entered the petition-making process itself. Simultaneously, an assessment of over a thousand petitions in the very years spanning the revolt of 1857—petitions that had originated in the different villages, towns and provinces of India—leads us to the not necessarily opposite belief that people as individuals often petitioned the government for a just review of a perceived wrong or for correcting administrative error with an authentic and honest motivation and, indeed, even an expectation of justice.[11] A trader from Lucknow in the throes of rebellion bewailed the loss of his goods in itinerant trade, shepherds from Ahmedabad pleaded against the forcible confiscation of their ghee (clarified butter), an English widow from Agra desired compensation from the government on her husband's death in military action against the rebels, and an accountant from Madras in the employ of the Company recounted the history of his loyal services since 1814 in order to be considered for a grant of land in 1857.[12]

Such affirmation of colonial power as well as the rejection of its legitimacy led to a phenomenal growth in the volume and amplitude of petition-making, so much so that by the last years of the Company's rule there is in evidence what may be called a thickening of the official record in this regard. This record stands as testimony to the greatly increasing importance of petition-making to British colonial state policy as well as to the involvement and participation of the laity in the determination of the character of British rule. According to this researcher's count for the years from before the revolt of

1857, to after the founding of the Indian National Congress in 1885, petitions presented to and considered by the highest level of offices of Governor-General, the Secretary of State and the Queen (from 1877 the Queen Empress) numbered between three hundred at the very least to over a thousand every year for an entire half century.[13]

The very numerousness of this partially extant record testifies the importance that both ruler and subject accorded it. The overwhelming presence in society of this mode of governance and communication constituted, as it were, the very core of a context around which ranged a diversity of cultural attitude and political mentality.

The petitioning process was put to many different uses. In one instance, notable for the fact that its author was an officer of the colonial police in Bombay, the petitioner desired of the government that they allow him to retain a particular commission that he had earned without the necessary official sanctions but with rare entrepreneurial verve through the supply of flotillas and related provisions as required in the organization of a police force in Sind for over a decade. This petitioner was supported in his plea by several testimonials, not only by certain superior associates of his former years of service but also by 315 of the principal "Merchants and Inhabitants" of Karachi. They made out a case for the retention of Colonel Marston as an officer in Sind and in standing witness to the essential nature of the expenses that the Bombay government desired that he should return to them by characterizing the society to which they belonged and which in their view Colonel Marston had helped to discipline, thus:

> ...the habits, customs, idiosyncrasies and predilections of the indigenous population are such as to distinguish it from every other race in India... and require being dealt within an exceptional way altogether.[14]

Of course, in the British view such a society could itself use the petitioning process to its own advantage. When, for example, in a small northern Indian town, a centre of Hindu pilgrimage, a tax was levied for the construction of new drains, the town's population led by a dominant trading family, downed shutters.

They argued against the tax in repeated meetings of their leaders with the local magistrate. These meetings resulted from a petition made by a person with an assumed name. Whole days were spent in locating this person. News of the unrest in the town disseminated widely by the indigenous vernacular newspapers of the region, reached the ears of the Viceroy through the press than through any conduit of government, a matter of some regret and eventual censure of the local and negligent magistrate who, it was lamented, had not paid sufficient heed to the petition. However, when, despite government reassurance that the tax would not be levied as it had been imposed rather arbitrarily, the unrest in the town did not die down, the Commissioner of the area had to camp out in the *mofussil* where he attempted to summon from the town the person in whose name the petition had originated. He met with much greater success than he may have hoped for. Many, "from all castes and classes", bore that name. He asked sixteen of the "better-known" among them if any of them was the author of the petition but each one of them disclaimed any knowledge of it whatsoever. Further confabulations and reiterated reassurances from the government followed. The town returned to normal. The petitioning process had yielded a victory as the drain tax mooted had been withdrawn. The tumult described in government record as a movement of "passive resistance" came to a close. But the petitioner could not be traced. Or at least that is how it appeared.[15]

The bracketed presence of a British police officer and Indian merchant (or inhabitant) in the same "cause" and an anonymous petition having a whole town in movement are but two instances of a combination of the many articulations of society around and through the petitioning process. Less striking manifestations of the wider permeation of the petitioning process in society and therefore as the expression of "society" itself are even more revealing. In the slow round of everyday life, the mentalities that lay behind notions of obligation, defiance and sovereignty came repeatedly to the fore.

A memorial in 1867 from Mohunt Srobun Doss, the head of a religious akhara at Sadduckbag in the District of Murshidabad in Bengal, had the state's revenue authorities preoccupied with the reckoning of the legitimacy and power of their own earlier decisions on the land grant of the temple establishment for long years, in the last instance since 1848. Srobun Doss' grant, that had originated in the Ranee Bhowanny's munificence in the pre-British Bengal of the villainous Nawab Sirajuddoulah in 1755, had been resumed by the colonial power, after having granted it a lease of life, in 1845. The memorialist presented the state's obligation to his institution not as the road-rolling of a pre-British customary right held by the grantee by the now dominant colonial state but as an instance of a continuity that derived from the fusion of the two kinds of power and custom, the British and the pre-British Nawabi or "Zamindari". This continuity was presented as the common consequence of the now melded notion of the social contract between what were once warring powers, a notion that`informed the thinking of the petitioner as much as it did that of the recipient.[16] The driving political and economic exigencies of the state in 1868 could not of course undo its own existence but the reviewing and debating of documents centred upon the question of state obligation as that derived from the acceptance of past powers clearly showed that mentalities across the great divide of 1857 insistently engaged the attention of the state on the tricky question of its own overtly unquestionable authority. The invoking of past histories took several forms. Junior collateral lineages of defeated and routed dynasties pined for being restored the dignity of being able to retain their ancestor's tombs and thereby carry on the rituals associated with the tombs. Repeatedly between 1869 and 1886, such anguish found its way into the petitioning process as in the case of the memorial of Nawab Abbas Mirza, the descendant of Nawab Arsh Manzil, buried at the Gulab Bari at Fyzabad. Noteworthy in this particular memorial was its gold-embossed form, an iconicity of presentation that seemed to insist that times gone by were in spirit coeval with the colonial present, and would continue to unsettle any easy repose.[17]

Even when the sources of political instability had been tamed, for times long after they spoke in voices of loyalty, apology and innocence in a way that served as reminder to the rulers of the impermanence of their own temporal power. The Wahabi rebellion had been defeated, its members tried and incarcerated. But the petitioning process enabled, as in the case of Amir Khan, a hide-merchant of Calcutta and an alleged "conspirator" among the Wahabis, a series of entreaties between 1864 and 1873, from himself, his wife, and his friends in Calcutta to reach a wider public, including the press. The judge of his first trying court, a court in whose judgement the initial form of the charges had refused to stick, was moved by the report of the petitions in the newspapers to put his own rather mitigating view of the matter on file once again, "so that it may be seen whenever any question about Amir Khan's sentence (came) up". Petitions thus assisted a tendency towards further retrospective review in the judiciary, in government and in the public mind.[18]

The petitioning process also made for the reminding of the colonial powers of its unfulfilled promises. In the case of Karamut Khan, a Resaldar of the Nagpur Irregular Cavalry (disbanded in 1862) we have one such instance. The state had rewarded him with a pension higher than what his rank would have fetched him for "shewing marked courage and fidelity to the Government" against the rebels of 1857 through a rare military action in which Karamut Khan saved his officer's life and boldly confronted a mutinous rebellion in his regiment, not fearing for his own life nor caring for the wound that resulted from his stance. Eleven years later Karamut Khan petitioned for a grant of land in addition to or in lieu of his "good service" pension. These claims were unacceptable to Government who considered that to "a soldier of this class land (would) prove... a questionable gift" that would entail a loss in its management and end finally in alienation. But in refusing their favour the Chief Commissioner presiding also added the further gratuitous observation that the petitioner's character "of late" had not been "altogether satisfactory" but, as was keenly remarked when the petition was considered a last time before it was finally rejected, it was "not stated in what respect the petitioner's conduct was found fault with".

This uncertainty of judgement arising from patently false and mixed motives that underpinned government action in Karamut Khan's case, may be seen to have determined, more generally, the consequences of such disavowals of faith into, first, a series of grumbles and then a more open questioning of the basis of colonial power itself.[19]

Like the formerly loyal, the suspected but unconvicted subjects of post-Mutiny India too seemed to have attempted to prize open the same space in government ambiguity through petitioning but in a demanding tone that Government should lift all suspicion from upon those who had not been convicted by its courts and in no case should they stand in the way of their finding employment if not in British India then in the India of the "princely state", under a Native Ruler. Maulvi Ally Kurreem berated the Government in a petition to the Viceroy thus:

> To be convicted as a rebel behind his back; — for all his property to be confiscated behind his back; to be refused a trial upon—Surrender on the express ground that there was no evidence forthcoming that could secure the conviction of your petitioner; to be debarred from earning a livelihood for himself and family in the service of the Rajahs and other landholders of the country, by the interference of the Government officials in the districts, interference not only private but openly conducted...
>
> Your petitioner may venture to say that in no country in the world, has a subject been treated by the government in the exceptional way in which your petitioner and his son has been... Had your petitioner been a convicted rebel—which he happily is not—he could not have been treated worse.[20]

Increasingly through the years the implied or explicit charge that the colonial government was not keeping to its word was made in petitions that had little to do with the question of the political legitimacy of the state *per se* but such petitions were argued out in that idiom.

Jadavray Harishankar, a *vakil* in the Kattyawar Agency Courts, in a petition from the Thana District Jail, accused his trying Judges and the governments of the Bombay Presidency and of India of having been unjustly prejudiced in determining his conviction. Significantly, he eventually related the question of the review of the judgement (for which he had petitioned) and its overruling by the Secretary of State to the general amnesty granted by the Empress of India at the assumption of that title by Queen Victoria. Jadavray Harishankar raised, as it were, a political objection, invoking a British act of mercy that was in fact also an act of the legitimation of Imperial rule against the colonial system of justice that he believed had been unfair to him.[21]

The theme of "unfairness" arising from an incidental recounting of a version of past sovereignty, again without directly addressing that question in terms of that of British rule itself, continued to be articulated in the petitioning process.

When the Government sought to bring a Bill to regulate the affairs of certain religious institutions by appointing a Central Board of Commissioners to oversee the management of temple grants in Madras Presidency, it was reminded by the Gnan Summuntha Pandara Sannathy, Mathathypathy or High Priest of the Tharmapooram Taluq Adheenum in the Mayaveram Taluq, Tanjore district, that the latter's and his ancestors' control over "27 Religious Institions and several Muttums" then under his Management had been "distinctly managed and superintended" competently "from a period long anterior to the assumption of the country by the British Government...". Arguing against the intention of giving the mooted Board of Commissioners "the power of alienating temple properties", he again reminded the state that "this was not even possessed by Government", of "serious consequences" that would follow if such an "arbitrary" power were to be conferred on any Board, that it would be a "breach of faith" relative to its own practices, "unfair", and above everything else would confirm that Government proposals were "as little to be depended on as those of the most changeable Eastern Rulers".[22]

This was below the belt, being compared to Oriental rulers, but the petitions also brought the soothing balm of the messages of loyalty, such as that of one Shah Muhammad Yaqub who petitioned for being granted a certificate of "good reputation" in the form of an address presented as a wedding present to the Duke and Duchess of York. The address itself was "a short family history" and it was sent along with a gold fish enclosed in a silver casket, and locked in an ebony box addressed to their Royal Highnesses. The burden of the short history was an intensely (and extensively) narrated story that began in Akbar's time when Yakub's ancestor was invited to the court of the Mughal Emperor. Thereafter, from one episode to another we see Yaqub's ancestors hurtling down the centuries until early British rule, ducking material benefits that fawning Mughal emperors from Akbar to Aurangzeb wished to honour them with, always scornful of the gifts of temporal power, and standing tall in spiritual self-esteem and revered religious learning. One whose ancestors had stood erect and tall in Mughal times now sought British favour by handing to them "a short history" "so that their Royal Highnesses may know the holiness of the Saints whose duct the fish contains."[23]

Sovereignty thus surrendered, in the ornate yet stark symbolism of the fish, was nevertheless being questioned from the most unexpected quarters. A British civilian, Mrs. Hearsey, in a petition to the Secretary of State, charged the British Government of India with having taken the Dun Valley in the Garhwal hills as early as 1811 from her grandfather who had bought the land from the Raja of Garhwal before the British conquest of the region. She wished that she now be given land or money in compensation for what was justly hers. That British conquest was itself so questioned was enough reason for the local government to hold back Mrs. Hearsey's petition, though they did it initially by the argument that she was merely seeking pecuniary assistance, and that petitions in that class of documents were not to be forwarded to the Secretary of State. When the petition was moved again in the early years of the twentieth century—not that Mrs. Hearsey was ever going to be obliged by the colonial state—it was finally turned down as now government was already gearing up its responses to the burgeoning challenge of Indain nationalism.[24]

There were also instances that spanned decades when

British sovereignty stood questioned. Petitions following successful litigation processes and in the depositions that followed the terms of colonial rule inevitably got involved with those of the earlier, customary, pre-British social contract. A banking firm claimed a debt due to it from a rebel of 1857, dead at the time of the final petition (made in 1881). The firm argued that it had made a loan under a registered deed to a certain Nawab who had later joined the rebels in the "mutiny" against the security of the Nawab's traditionally conferred pre-British endowments (and income therefrom) that the colonial government was unwilling to recognize. The government, finally rejecting the petition argued that were it not for the grant of a pension to the queen of a deposed ruler under the terms of "rulers' treaties" that in the margins the colonial state had decided to acknowledge as mariting its largesse, such a claim based on the debts of a banking firm owed to it from subsidiary land grants that did not inherit a similar privilege would never have arisen.[25]

The petition and the basis of its rejection were therefore constant reminders of the state's rule of force—described in another document as "a despotism tempered by petition"—and made the government examine closely the nature of the "extra-petition" links that such loyal documents might have had. In their opinion government, as late as 1888, "grievously lack(ed) information" and could afford to disregard "no means of ascertaining what is passing in the minds of men, whether by memorials, by Public meetings, or by the Press...".[26] As petitions often moved out of their narrow groove of "the proper channel" into finding resonances in society at large, government was equally wary of such resonances finding links that might solidify into horizontal solidarities of class, community or nation and so strove zealously to keep its bureaucracy free from this contagion.

It simply and directly banned the receipt of congratulatory addresses and/or presents, by members of the bureaucracy from the native community in the belief that at the felicitatory functions for this purpose, views would be and were expressed, (and reported by the press) by both the members of the "Native Community" and by the retiring or being transferred civil servants in their vote of thanks that might contribute indirectly to the stoking of sentiments and mentalities that were altogether unfavourable to British rule.[27]

While this is the subject of another discussion, it may be said that the government reprimanded at least a half-dozen of its officers for violating the rule; and many others who pleaded ignorance of the rule. Government believed such addresses to be "seldom the spontaneous act of the community"[28] and viewed their placement in the interstices between petitions and memorials to (or when to higher authority, through) them as potentially fraught with possibilities of the worst kind. As directly stated in an instance of the condoning of one such "exceptional" case: "The presentation of addresses, even from persons at a distance, *might encourage political agitation* and lead to other objectionable consequences."[29] (emphasis added) Four years following the preceding instance, the Lieutenant-Governor of a province recommended to the Government of India that a "Portrait Painter" had done a small portrait of a District and Sessions Judge who might be allowed, at his retirement, to accept the painting as a small felicitating gift from the painter.[30] This was disallowed. The Raj was resolute in its conviction that it must stand apart from the very people whose petitions it entertained.

Let us return to the institutional history of petitioning. In the decades 1855 to 1895, over which we have just reviewed the contents of petitions made to the Government and the implications of the different acts in the personages involved, the political messages exposed, and the mentalities revealed, petition writing itself became a form of expression.

We have already alluded to its numerousness over the years. As the years went by, persons writing their petitions increased in number until such time as the Government of several provinces seriously considered containing what was beginning to be seen as a growing scourge. Rules were made and put into force in some of these provinces while in others it was thought impolitic to do so. Urging the "proper control and supervision of the practice of petition-writers", one senior official observed, "Their (the petition writers') ways are dark and crooked and outside the open cognizance of the courts". Another commented on his experience as a member of a Presidency Council: "When in... Council, I ordered that the writer of the petition should invariably sign his name and give his residence or the petition would not be received". According to him, this "had a good effect on the substance (emphasis in original) of the petitions".[31]

The rules moved from forbidding the forwarding of "improperly worded" and "disrespectful" petitions to include, by the early 1890s, "disloyal" as well. As petitions grew to coming "exceedingly aggressive" and "insubordinately worded" in tone, certain members of the bureaucracy began to regard the management of these as of so much trivia, while the British Parliament, at the turn of the century, at the instance of an individual member, asked for a tabulated statement of all the petitions withheld and with what cause over a five-year period.[32] Clearly there was a ground-swell as petitioning itself became the very content of its own form. But we must not hurry to conclude from this that the politics of petitioning took control of the mentalities it represented. If the Madras Government refused to forward a petition to Parliament from a community pleading that the "so-called" Indian National Congress[33] must not be considered a representative organization of the Indian people, nor was a petition, utterly economic nationalist in content, on the adverse effects of the adjusted rupee-sterling ratio relative to the price of silver, forwarded by the Secretary of State to the Parliament.[34] The connection between mentality histories, the petitioning process and early Indian nationalism was more complex. That is what I have suggested. It has been the burden of my argument that petitioning in colonial India not merely facilitated the expression of anguish and dissent and indeed even aspiration among the laity, but made way for the emergence of the eventually overtly articulated nationalistic resolution. From a haltingly expressed harking to fully formed but socially receding notions of sovereignty, this very petitioning process, by the last quarter of the nineteenth century stood transformed, into a statement of ideology.

THE BRITISH HISTORICAL CONTEXT

To turn now to the British historical context, albeit briefly. Petitioning in Britain has a long history but this process itself was earlier considered a "secret" privilege of Parliament. The contents of petitions made to Parliament could not be divulged to the laity. The English Civil War had broken the back of this secrecy as did the wider dissemination of the contents of petitions through signed and anonymous printing. Thus petitioning dove-tailed into the process of the creation of the public sphere, not necessarily in an Enlightenment-driven rationality as may have been true for the eighteenth century but more simply as a feature of a wider sphere of debate driven by the assertion of rights and grievances.[35] It may be useful to recall here that the construction of the Leviathan had preceded the fullest eventual development of capitalism and the creation of the modern middle-class nation-state in British society. Indeed, even the final and eventual forging of the nation was completed specially in the century that marked the years before 1840.[36]

Petitioning in British society, then, had arrived in the tumultuous years of the appearance of the seventeenth century Leviathan and became transformed, through the myriad processes of the creation of a nation and the fruition of capitalism, into a conduit of social and political articulation that did not by itself, on its own, signify the crystallization of the modern state. Rather, whether it was the mass petitioning against Catholic emancipation (1829) or the monster petitions of the Chartist Movement (1837-1848), petitioning in Britain in the modern centuries, both during and after the industrial revolution, sought always to reaffirm the people's desires, individually or collectively, by appealing to a state, a nation-state, the prior existence and political significance of which, as authority-giver and norm-protector, was readily assumed. To illustrate this truth of the British state being considered by those who petitioned it to be a protector of rights and norms in a variety of spheres of social life, let us look at a few examples from the British archives.

But first a methodological note. The history of petitioning in Britain is a historically established reality and we do not presume in the examples we look at presently to be offering a slice of any social history of that society. The examples offered here illustrate how, in the most general of subjects, as diverse and variegated as ecclesiastical legitimacy, medical research, public disaffection, and others, the relationship of the petitioner to the British state, even when questioning or qualifying governmental action, was always affirming of the principles and norms that integrated state and society in nineteenth century Britain.

PETITIONING IN BRITAIN

The assertion of widely acceptable standards of social practice and norms of the nation was perhaps best exemplified in the necessity that the apex bodies of medical science in Britain saw of reforming the law concerned with the dissection of human cadavers. As late as the years 1831 and 1832, by which date it was required by Parliament itself that all medical students must have "an intimate acquaintance with practical Anatomy, the surest basis on which the scienced practice of Medicine can be founded,"[37] we find "the Master, Wardens and Society of the Art and Mystery of Apothecaries of the City of London" and "The President and Commonalty of the Faculty of Physic in London", both, in separate petitions, appealing to the State for a law that would make the availability of cadavers for anatomical dissection a simple legal process in a civil society that was subordinated to the protocols of science. These bodies appealed in their petitions, "in the interest solely of knowledge", that their members ought not to have to transact with "the Vilest Class of Society" only through whose illegal trafficking in cadavers could the science of anatomy grow. But, even more significantly, they argued that "besides the considerations which more especially affect the medical profession the *public security* no less demands an immediate alteration of the present (illegal) system..." (emphasis added). The needs of the modern state, the interest of the public and that of science as knowledge itself (as well as bourgeois disdain for the "vilest class(es) of society") could all thus be brought together in these remarkable petitions that asserted all at once the many norms that served to integrate state and society in modern Britain.

Of course, not all petitions captured the convergence of issues as eloquently as those of the captains of medical science. But even petitions with a wholly sectional interest more often than not lodged their appeal within the terms of the nation and the generally accepted notion of the social good, thereby reaffirming the hegemony of the British state over the society over which it presided. "Silk Throwsters of the borough of Macclsefield," when asking for protective duties for their trade, invoked the welfare of "our Nation" : "We are Freeborn Englishmen ... Many of us have fought the Battles of our Beloved and Revered Sovereign and of our country in distant climes ...",[38] while "Noblemen and Gentlemen, Heritors of the Country of Roxburgh" felt it to be their duty which they owed "to Ourselves, Our Tenants and the interests of Our Country" to petition "against the law prohibiting the Distillation of Spirits from grain."[39] A "Memorial" from the Country of Warwick's "cultivators of the soil and growers of Wool" linked the adverse impact of imports to diminished employment and loss of wages to agricultural labourers, speaking of "alarming injury to our national prosperity", as did petitions on the same subject from Glamorgan, Gloucester, Norfolk, Somerset, Derbyshire and other areas.[40]

Even when a petition was as clearly frenetic as one from "a lady of little education" from Portsmouth, its contents were argued in terms of certain presumed dangers posed to the state in Britain. This lady claimed that she knew of a conspiracy of the French to "Invade us quietly" with many insidious devices. These included "Bastardism", the alleged tendency among the French of begetting illegitimate children, with which they might be expected to swamp Britain and "to weaken the State" itself.[41]

The petitions affirming the general social good and

respectful of the established social hierarchy are numerous and many be restated in an elaborated version at a later date. Suffice it to say here that even in petitions that defended the "rioters" and "incendiarists" of the great social tumult of the twenties and thirties of the nineteenth century, raised to iconic status in the social history of Great Britain,[42] the petitioners nearly always asserted that theirs were conditions made miserable by unfortunate circumstances, largely by poor administration, or as was stated by Thomas Attwood on behalf of the "incendiarists" up for trial: "we respectfully submit to your Majesty ... that the wrongs, difficulties and distresses of Your Majesty's faithful and loyal people have been occasioned by the *maladministration of public affairs*"[43] (emphasis in original). In this the Birmingham Political Union was not an exception and revolt and rebellion in Britain indeed threw up many a "loyal" resolution in the form of petitions that for the greater part underwrote the acceptability of that very social order within which the disaffection was manifest.

The kind of petition that did not emerge from a sectional, professional or disaffected class interest did of course have the emblematic mark of the integrated nation-state, as may be expected, even more firmly embossed upon it. For example, the idea of national progress was reiterated in a series of petitions over thirteen consecutive years from Thomas Gray for a plan of National Railway construction that he wished Government to support.[44] The idea of the nation could also be suborned in prayer as was pleaded for in a petition from the Inhabitants Dumfries and its vicinity for a day of fasting against pestilence and disease.[45] It could also recur in the same idiom from individual petitioners as from a carpenter who was himself the son of an inn-keeper and who petitioned in favour of "all classes and denominations as well as ages" so that the distressed artisans be helped and all of "The Industrious and honest classes of his Majesties (sic) dutiful subjects may be effected without delay."[46]

The "rights" of "loyal subjects" could also be asserted forcefully to get the state to, as it were, do its duty, to acknowledge these and codify the norms. Petitions supported the Reform Bill[47] and passionately urged the abolition of slavery in Britain's colonial possessions all over the world.[48] A prayer could also be written out and recommended to the entire country as a petition of thanksgiving for the final suppression of the Indian Rebellion[49] of 1857 and the saving of the Indian people, by God's grace, from the darknesses of their own society.

Our generalization will bear one final illustration from the randomly chosen but always generally applicable instances of harking to state power for the common good of the people of Britain, and not only of Britain. A petitioner pleaded for the colonizing of Madagascar so that universal Christian values espoused by all denominations of missionary work, "slave-extinction", "Aborigines protection", maritime ascendancy, free trade, "free-labour trade", "a market of British enterprise and manufacture", and "native usefulness" could all result from that act.[50]

The forging of the nation incorporated the popular will. It ratified state power and endorsed the legitimacy of government action.

CONCLUSION

We began this lecture by emphasizing the importance of petitioning in India, a process much too ignored until now. This process, we argued, reflected a groundswell of subcontinental attitudes that by the end of the nineteenth century were being converted to becoming an ideological statement, finally of Indian nationalism in its many heterogeneous manifestations within that particular collectivity. As the government was British and the attitudes and stances Indian, these were not integrated with one another. But petitioning was a conduit in which, and through which, the people addressed an alien state usually by harking back to the past in the process of claiming what they believed to be theirs in the contemporaneous present.

We then looked briefly at the history of Britain and found petitioning there to have been less central in the making of the nation and the nation-state as these latter phenomena were already secured, structured and, as it were, in place by the late eighteenth century. We followed this up with a review of petitions in British society based on archival foragings and were confirmed in our view that the place of the state and the nation was already that of the norm-giver by that time. Neither the state nor the nation emerged from petitioning as significantly as each of these phenomena did in colonial India.

Contrasting the Indian instance with the British leads us, then, to some arguably plausible conclusions. The substance and form of petitioning in colonial India was integral to the representativeness of the Indian populace in its response to British rule. Whatever continuities of Indian society persisted through the two centuries of British rule were in fact made articulate only within the process of the creation of the British colonial state and government. Put differently, were it not for the colonial bureaucracy of an alien government that had its own goals to meet, the multitude of voices in the petitioning process may not have found politically significant expression at all. Thus the argument for considering continuities in modern Indian history makes sense only when these are seen as determined by British rule, not despite it.[51]

Unlike in the British instance, if it be allowed that petitioning in colonial India was of foundational significance for the eventual emergence of the Indian nation and state, then this cannot in any sense have been derivative.[52] As we have seen, the many asserted values of the petitions in the colonial era were not derived from the British historical experience at all, especially when we consider that the experiene of the two respective contexts of Britain and India, can hardly be considered comparable, in even the remotest degree on account of their different mindsets and political, social and economic structure. An altogether different setting of the terms of reference would be needed to recognize the Indian experience, not the one in which it is described in an implicitly but mistakenly comparative way as "incomplete", "partial", or, for that matter, "distorted".[53]

I seek the indulgence of the audience in raising this question.

REFERENCE

1. The historical accounts on which this is based are by S.R. Mehrotra, Anil Seal and Bipan Chandra, among others. The story of peasant risings may be found in a compendium edited by A.R. Desai.
2. Peasant responses have been interpreted best, but also most tendentiously, by Ranjit Guha while in Bipan Chandra's work the social basis of the intelligentsia's economic nationalist response cries out for delineation.
3. By Dipesh Chakrabarty, primarily.
4. To call these"fragments", as Partha Chatterjee does, does not resolve the issue.
5. A large body of published and unpublished recent works in Indian, British and North American universities and research institutes, too numerous to be detailed.
6. Precis of Correspondence regarding the Transmission of Memorials or Petitions addressed to the Home Authorities. Proceedings 237-A, Home Public Records, Aug. 1867, National Archives of India.
7. *Ibid.*
8. *Ibid.*
9. *Ibid.*
10. *Ibid.* Also programmes 237 and 238 of the same year.
11. Diary of Petitions, entries for 1854-1856 and 1857-1859, Home Miscellaneous, Nos. 545 & 585. NAI. These are bound volumes of an independently retained record.
12. Entries as recorded, "Diaries", cited above.
13. This count is of just the one set of proceedings, the Home Public, and covers "Addresses", "Memorials" and "Petitions". This series, the Home Public, has the most extensive index for this subject and may therefore also be considered in many ways, truly representative.
14. Petition of Colonel Edward Chanles Marston, Home Public Records, 1873, NAI.
15. Papers relating to the petition of Muttra Das, Home Public Records, 1864, NAI.
16. Petition of Mohunt Srobun Das, Home Public Records, 1868, NAI.
17. Petition of Nawab Abbas Mirza, Home Public Records, 1886, NAI.
18. Petition of Amir Khan, Home Public Records, 1873, 1875, 1976, NAI.

19. Petition of Karamut Khan, Home Public Records, 1874, NAI.
20. Petition of Moulvi Ally Kurreem, Home Public Records, 1873, NAI.
21. Petition of Jadavray Harishankar, Home Public Records, 1880, NAI.
22. Petition of Gnan Summuntha Pandara Sannathy, Tanjore, Home Public Records, 1880 NAI.
23. Petition of Shah Muhammad Yaqub, Home Public Records, 1894, NAI.
24. Petition of Mrs. Hearsey, Home Public Records, 1914, NAI.
25. Petition of a banking firm, Home Public Records, 1881, NAI.
26. Papers on the undesirability of the acceptance of petitions by public servants, Home Public Records, 1882, 1884, 1888, NAI.
27. *Ibid.*
28. *Ibid.*
29. *Ibid.*
30. Petition for permission to a judge due for retirement to accept a portrait of himself, Home Public Records, 1887 NAI.
31. Notes on the control of petition writing, Home Public Records, 1889 NAI.
32. Correspondence, Government of India and the Government of Bombay, on the withholding of petitions, Home Public Records, 1895, NAI.
33. Petition by the Kammalahs of Southern India, Home Public Records, 1895, NAI.
34. Petition on this subject to the Secretary of State, Home Public Records, 1894, NAI.
35. David Zaret, "Petitions and the 'Invention' of Public Opinion in the English Revolution", *American Journal of Sociology,* Vol. 101, No. 6, May 1996, pp. 1497-1555.
36. Linda Colley, *Forging the Nation 1707-1837,* Yale University Press, 1992.
37. Petition Civil, A., No. 54/4, to the Rt. Hon'ble Lord Viscount Melbourne, Dec. 1831, Home Office Record, P.R.O., Kew and 1832 Petitions P., Home Office Record 54/5, P.R.O., Kew.
38. Petition, 22 December 1825, Board of Trade Record, 6/176, one among many such; and from Tanners and Shoemakers, May 1803 & c., BTR BT 6/178, Memorial of Paper Stainers 20 Feb., 1817 "on the evils of Stancelling (sic)", BTR BT 6/174.
39. Petition dated 31 Oct. 1810, BTR BT 6/177.
40. Memorial dated 24 April, 1819, BTR BT 6/173 and including Derbyshire high peak scarsdale and high peak Agricultural

Society's memorial and printed resolution April, 1819.

41. Memorial dated 24 October, 1821 from Caroline Barrett, Portsmouth, Portsea, Hants., HO 44/10 folio 7, pp. 25-26.
42. Especially in the exceptional and groundbreaking work of Eric Hobsbawm and George Rude.
43. The HumblePetition of the Council of the Birmingham Political Union, dated 5 October 1831, Petitions Civil A-1831. HO 54/H.
44. Petitions G, 1832 from Thomas Gray, dated 22 Nov. 1832. HO 54/5.
45. Petition for "National Fast" in Petitions D 1832, dated 18 January 1832. HO 54/5.
46. Petition dated 25 May 1835 from Devon, HO 44/17.
47. Document with enclosure, report on large public meeting in support of Reform Bill, Haddington, ref. The same as in note 43, above.
48. Memorial 12 April 1833, HO 54/7, Petitions.
49. Appeal to have a thanksgiving text to this effect read out in all chapels and churches. HO 45 OS6857.
50. Printed Memorial from Henry Ibbotson to Her Majesty's Secretary for the British Colonies, 1841, re: Madagascar, HO 54/35.
51. This must qualify Chris Bayly's emphasis on continuities in Indian history from precolonial times to the early twentieth century.
52. This must qualify Partha Chatterjee's assertion on nationalist 'discourse'.
53. These were much used terms drawn from a primarily Marxist, but also liberal, engagement with the subject, especially in the seventies.

Acknowledgement and Caveat

The Charles Wallace Fund made it possible for me to use the P.R.O. Archives at Kiev in June 2000 and the JNU supported sabbatical leave in 1996. This lecture is culled from ongoing work. Fuller references will be provided in future publication.